Clifton Park - Halfmoon Public Library

Pebble®

Horses

Arabian Horses

by Erin Monahan

Consulting Editor: Gail Saunders-Smith, PhD

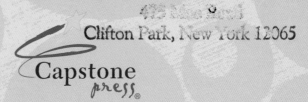

Capstone
press®

Mankato, Minnesota

Pebble Books are published by Capstone Press,
151 Good Counsel Drive, P.O. Box 669, Mankato, Minnesota 56002.
www.capstonepress.com

1 2 3 4 5 6 14 13 12 11 10 09

Library of Congress Cataloging-in-Publication Data
Monahan, Erin, 1977–
    Arabian horses / by Erin Monahan.
    p. cm. — (Pebble Books. Horses)
    Includes bibliographical references and index.
    Summary: "A brief introduction to the characteristics, life cycle, and uses of
the Arabian horse breed"— Provided by publisher.
    ISBN-13: 978-1-4296-2233-2 (hardcover)
    ISBN-10: 1-4296-2233-4 (hardcover)
    1. Arabian horse — Juvenile literature. I. Title.
SF293.A8M66 2009
636.1'12 — dc22   4463   2008026820

Note to Parents and Teachers

The Horses set supports national science standards related to
life science. This book describes and illustrates Arabian horses.
The images support early readers in understanding the text.
The repetition of words and phrases helps early readers learn new
words. This book also introduces early readers to subject-specific
vocabulary words, which are defined in the Glossary section. Early
readers may need assistance to read some words and to use the
Table of Contents, Glossary, Read More, Internet Sites, and Index
sections of the book.

Table of Contents

Beautiful Arabians 5

From Foal to Adult 13

Riding Arabians. 17

Glossary 22

Read More 23

Internet Sites. 23

Index 24

4

Beautiful Arabians

The Arabian is the oldest breed of horse.
The first Arabians came from deserts in southwestern Asia.

6

Arabian horses are known
for their beauty.
They have long, curved necks.
Their faces curve inward
below their eyes.

black

gray

bay

chestnut

8

Arabians have silky coats. Most Arabians are black, gray, bay, or chestnut.

withers

10

Arabians are smaller than
many other horse breeds.
Most Arabians stand
14 to 15.3 hands high.

Horses are measured in hands.
Each hand is 4 inches (10 centimeters).
A horse is measured from the ground
to its withers.

12

From Foal to Adult

Female Arabians give birth to one foal at a time. Arabian foals are fearless and learn quickly.

Arabians aren't ridden
until they are
about 2 years old.
Most Arabians live
25 to 30 years.

Riding Arabians

Arabians have a smooth trot. They can travel a long way without getting tired.

Arabians are smart
and learn quickly.
Their gentle nature makes
them good riding horses.

Owners brush and ride
their Arabians often.
Owners enjoy spending time
with their beautiful horses.

Glossary

bay — brown with a black mane and tail

breed — a certain kind of animal within an animal group; Arabians are a breed of horse.

chestnut — a red-brown color

coat — the hair covering a horse's body

foal — a young horse or pony

nature — an animal's personality

silky — shiny and soft

trot — to move at a quick speed; trotting is faster than walking but slower than galloping.

Read More

Dell, Pamela. *Arabians.* Majestic Horses. Chanhassen, Minn.: Child's World, 2007.

Pitts, Zachary. *The Pebble First Guide to Horses.* Pebble First Guides. Mankato, Minn.: Capstone Press, 2009.

Internet Sites

FactHound offers a safe, fun way to find educator-approved Internet sites related to this book.

Here's what you do:

1. Visit *www.facthound.com*
2. Choose your grade level.
3. Begin your search.

This book's ID number is 9781429622332.

FactHound will fetch the best sites for you!

Index

brushing, 21
coats, 9
deserts, 5
eyes, 7
faces, 7
foals, 13
gentle, 19

learning, 13, 19
necks, 7
owners, 21
riding, 15, 19, 21
size, 11
smart, 19
trotting, 17

Word Count: 141
Grade: 1
Early-Intervention Level: 16

Editorial Credits
Erika L. Shores, editor; Bobbi J. Wyss, designer;
    Sarah L. Schuette, photo shoot direction

Photo Credits
All photos by Capstone Press/TJ Thoraldson Digital Photography

The Capstone Press Photo Studio thanks Cedar Ridge Arabians and Diane Fralish
for their help with photo shoots.

Capstone Press thanks Robert Coleman, PhD, associate professor of
Equine Extension at the University of Kentucky, Lexington's Department
of Animal Sciences, for reviewing this book.